I0484684

This is my gift to you!

I am dedicating this book to those who are struggling in this economy. Those who think there is no solution available for retirement I am telling you there are perfectly good solutions waiting for you. This is my thanks to your family for making this country great. If you have or are trying to save money for your retirement I am telling you there are solutions available. All you have to do is look at the right places. From experience I am telling you that if you have money saved up in your retirement account it is time to preserve and grow. If you are few years away from retirement you still have hope. Just have faith.

Thank you for reading this book and passing it on to your friends.

"My wife and I first met Ash about two and a half years ago at a seminar he gave on having a Safe and Secure Retirement. Since then we put our retirement accounts with him. Based on our experiences with stock market declines over the years, first with a large brokerage house and then with a major bank handling our investments, we wish we had met Ashish earlier. Our contracts have shown no losses during the downward market movements. It is particularly important to us to preserve our principle since we have reached retirement age. Also, our contracts are set up to provide us lifetime income while capturing upside potential without experiencing market losses. Ashish has given us personal attention and has been available when we needed to consult with him ever since he started handling our retirement. We view him as a friend as well as a specialist.

We believe he is genuinely concerned about our financial future and we look forward to a long relationship with him."

-Frank and Judi H. Woodstock, MD-

No Nonsense Retirement Academy

Find all the facts, eliminate any fiction, and go from unsecured retirement to Safe and Secure retirement.

Look you have been through lot in life! You have paid your dues; been through some rough financial situations; rode ups and downs in the market in your lifetime; and you have seen different political climates; Have more gray hair, and that makes you a wise person. After all you are the reason this country flourished. You took companies like Gerber baby food from thousands of jars to Millions of jars being sold. Because of you Mattel, Fisher-Price, Hasbro, McDonald's, Pizza hut, Burger king, and industries such as Real estate, and financial services have boomed. Because of your frugal habits we are better off.

And now it is time for you to retire with peace of mind. You deserve to have a safe and secure retirement. You deserve to be free from the volatility of the markets, and have a Worry Free Retirement.

What you don't need are worries, headaches, and sleepless nights. What you do need are solutions that are safe and secure. As a Retirement Phase Specialists I can help you weed out the Fiction and bring the Facts to the table. What you need is a person who can help you go from unsecure to safe and secure retirement. What you need is a path that you can follow and a guide who can help you get there safely and securely.

That is why I have written this E-Book. In this book you will find No More Nonsense.
You will discover that some of the beliefs you had were just a fiction and will discover true facts.

NOTES

The Results

My clients have been able to save thousands of dollars in the past market crash because, they decided to stop the bleeding from the stock market, and applied the insured retirement solutions. They decided to get out of Buy, Hold, and Pray strategies. Instead they decided to plan with Insured Retirement Solution; Capture upside, and never have to worry about the down turn of the market ever again. My clients who have been with me since 2004 are not only able to keep their principal safe and secure, but they have been able to preserve the market index gains captured before the 2008 market crash. Thus In the 2008

market crash my clients lost $0
and kept all their principal and
gains.

By implementing insured
retirement solutions they saved
money on their Social Security
Taxation, Avoided probate,
reduced taxes on interest
income, and been guaranteed a
lifetime income which they
cannot outlive.

This is a real possibility for you
as well. But first you need to
take some simple steps in order
to achieve the goal of having
safe and secure retirement.

YOUR GOALS

PROBLEMS/ROADBLOCKS

The first step in achieving your goal is to understand the problems that you are facing today. This country is facing the biggest economic crisis. There are real issues that need to be solved before the turning point.

Fiction
Government Reported Debt
$14,000,000,000,000
www.usdebtclock.org

Fact
Real debt of US
$74,000,000,000,000
http://www.Truthin2010.org

Let me put it in simple terms. If you can spend $750,000 per day for 2,000 years. You would be half way to $1,000,000,000,000. If you stack $100 bills next to each other the line would go 1,200 miles long.

The US government has only 2 choices.

1. Increase their income
2. Decrease spending

Guess, which one they are choosing? You are right they are choosing to increase the income from the taxpayers. The government is actively looking at that being the solution.

This is one of the reasons causing the markets to go up and down. Basically it is uncertain which way US outlook is headed. You can see that even S&P downgraded US ratings to AA+. This causes issues for you. You are facing serious obstacles. There is a strong possibility that the market could go down and may never recover. So my question to you is how much volatility can you handle? How long can you wait for market recovery? And how many times can you afford to loose 50% of your portfolio?

YOUR THOUGHTS

Facts about clients

Before they met us though they were struggling just like you. They had serious worries about their retirement. They were worried about the volatility of the market, running out of money, Taxes, Debt, and Probate. But the difference was they choose to take action;

1. They choose to order our Free Found Facts Report.
2. They found out the facts about their situation and eliminated the fiction.

3. They choose to take action and get out the way of the storm that was coming.

That is what saved them from the last down turn of 2008.
My clients who have been with me since 2004 have lost $0 because they chose to do two things;

1. They choose to get our Free Found Facts Report.

2. Implement insured retirement Solutions provided by the Insured Retirement Solutions Providers. With our help they choose A+ rated carriers, who has billions in assets, 120%+ reserves, 150%+ liquidity, and have been around for a long time.

My question to you is are you prepared for the next downturn?

Yes
NO

Clients, Problems, Solutions

In 1994 when I started in the financial services industry I did not know about these solutions. But ever since 2004 I started to work with Boomers, and retirees, safe money I became a Retirement Phase Specialist. In my quest to finding a safe and secure solutions, I have found these Insured Retirement Solutions through Insured Retirement Solution Providers.

My clients suffered significant market losses before they met me. My clients wanted to eliminate the down side risk, reduce or eliminate Social Security Taxation, Reduce taxes on interest income, avoid probate, and Not run out of money at old age. They were running significant risk of running out of money because they were not safe and secure. They were trying to preserve as much as they could but because they were working with **Accumulation Phase Advisors** they were not able to get the right solution for them.

As a Retirement Phase Specialist I am able to:
- Eliminate 100% downside risk from market losses

- Capture 100%+ up side of the market indexes credits in writing.
- Possibly eliminate taxes on social security income, and even interest income.
- Bypass probate
- Capture upside of the credited index gains
- Eliminate downside risk from the market.
- Have a lifetime income that they won't outlive.

WHO WOULD YOU RATHER WORK WITH?

GENERALIST

OR

SPECIALIST

A STORY of SUCCESS

I have clients who came to me in 2009 for some help with their non-retirement money in the bank. With a simple goal of Not loosing money in the market and reducing taxes on their interest income. We mutually agreed to put major portion of their money in the Insured Retirement Solution with a Insured Retirement Provider who had an A+ rating before and after the crash. Has 130% reserves, and 169% liquidity. Because of this they have had double digit index credits, which is guaranteed to not go down ever again. We have eliminated taxes from their interest income and have saved them close to thousand dollars per year. And have given them Guaranteed lifetime income, which they cannot outlive.

I have a client in their mid 60's who came to me in 2004 and wanted to protect his principle, gains and bypass probate. Him and his wife gave me significant portion of their portfolio. The husband passed away about a year ago. We were able to bypass probate for her and have successfully captured the gains and preserved both principle and gains from the market losses.

I have a client in there 60's who came to me in 2008 right around the crash. They were with a major Brokerage house. They had lost more then 50% of their portfolio in 2001 crash. So this time they were determined to not do that again. Looking at their account they discovered that they were paying 3 – 5% in fees on their account.

With their portfolio of mid six figures this came to be a significant amount. They also found out that they were at 100% risk if the market went down again. With both of them nearing retirement in 3 – 5 years they were also afraid that they would outlive their money especially if the market went down. After we mutually agreed to put all of their retirement money in safe and secure place. 10% went into their bank savings for immediate needs and 90% went into Insured Retirement Solution. Today, because of the Insured

Retirement Solutions they were able to preserve their entire retirement captured index interest gains, as a result they are more confident and prepared for their retirement.

I have a client who was age 65 who came to me in Dec. 2008. Wanting to not loose his principle and Gains. He wanted to Bypass probate, reduce taxes on Social Security Income, Pass the money on to his heirs, and have a lifetime income if he choose in 3 years or so. He gave me almost seven figures. Today because of the Insured Retirement Solutions We have been able to do Preserve his Principle & Gains, By pass probate, have money set in a way that he can pass it on to his heirs, and have a lifetime income any time he wants. The only thing we could not do is help him with Social Security income because him and his wife still earn well over six figures income.

All this is possible for you as well. Just ask us for our **FREE Found Fact Report** and we will eliminate Fiction and bring out the Facts.

All of these people requested to have a **FREE Found Fact Report.** This is a 2 page report which will bring out all the **facts** to the table so you can make an intelligent decision about your situation. During our fact-finding process we discovered their goals and dreams they wanted to accomplish. Of course understanding clients and their needs is a vital task that we have. Understanding your needs and wants is our job. If you are looking to not loose money, Insured retirement solutions may be the right fit for you. You should work with a Retirement Phase Specialist to get the most favorable solution for you.

WHAT ARE YOUR
TOP 3 GOALS FOR YOUR
RETIREMENT?

1.

2.

3.

"I first met Ashish in 2009 through a very close friend who had attended one of his No Nonsense Retirement Academies educational event. I had been troubled by the continuing decrease in my retirement accounts that were in stocks and mutual funds. I asked Ashish to look over my portfolio and help me with a solution. After two years, in spite of the fall in the market, I have been able to protect 100% my principle and credited interest gains. I am pleased that I have been able to protect both my principle and captured interest gains. Today my money not only protected but I have seen a significant increase in my contracts captured interest gains. Now I feel safe and secure about my retirement. I now am able to sleep well at night knowing retirement fund are growing while being protected. I have been very satisfied with the change I made and I am happy to say that I'm so glad to have met, Ashish. Thanks you!"

- Linda O. Owings Mills MD -

Think of 3 friends or family members who could benefit from this book and give it to them.

1.

2.

3.

Call Me for your FREE Found Fact Report today.

(O) 410-814-7570

NoNonsenseRetirementAcademy

mailto:Ash@NoNonsenseRetirementAcademy.com

Who Is Ash?

http://www.AshIsCash.com

Ash@AshIsCash.com